PASSENGER TRAINS

TRAINS

Lynn M. Stone

The Rourke Corporation, Inc.
Vero Beach, Florida 32964

© 1999 The Rourke Corporation, Inc.

PHOTO CREDITS:
Cover, p. 4, 17, 21 © Lynn M. Stone; title page, p. 10, p. 12-13 from East West
Rail Scenes; p. 7 © Jerry Hennen; p. 15 © Don Hennen; p. 8 by Al Regan/George
H. Drury Collection; p. 18 © George H. Drury

PRODUCED BY:
East Coast Studios, Merritt Island, Florida

EDITORIAL SERVICES:
Penworthy Learning Systems

Library of Congress Cataloging-in-Publication Data

Stone, Lynn M.
     Passenger trains / by Lynn M. Stone
        p. cm. — (Trains)
     Summary: Describes the history and uses of passenger trains, the different
types, and some famous ones.
     ISBN 0-86593-518-1
     1. Railroads—Trains Juvenile literature. 2. Railroads—United States—History
Juvenile literature 3. Railroads—Passenger-cars Juvenile literature.
[1. Railroads—Trains] I. Title. II. Series: Stone, Lynn M. Trains.
TF148.S88 1999
385'.22'0973—dc21   99-13203
                                                                            CIP

Printed in the USA

TABLE OF CONTENTS

PASSENGER TRAINS

Passenger trains travel over railroad tracks and carry people from place to place.

People ride in the train's passenger cars. Most passenger cars have several rows of seats. Other passenger cars have special areas for eating, sleeping, or playing games.

Passenger trains that travel only between large cities and the nearby towns, called **suburbs** (SUB erbz), are **commuter** (kuh MEU ter) trains.

Intercity (IN ter SIT ee) trains carry passengers long distances, sometimes across the entire United States or Canada.

Three of every four train passengers in the U.S. ride commuters like this Chicago-to-Aurora train.

EARLY PASSENGER TRAINS

The first regular passenger service in the U.S. began in 1831 on the Baltimore & Ohio Railroad. The first B & O trains didn't travel far or fast, but rail travel improved quickly.

In the early days, passengers traveled in uncomfortable wooden cars. By the late 1860s, however, long-distance trains had fancy sleeping cars, dining cars, and parlor cars. In parlor cars, people could play cards, relax, and visit in comfort.

For nearly the first 105 years of passenger service, Americans rode behind steam locomotives.

The Santa Fe Railroad's magnificent Chief leaves Chicago in 1968, shortly before the Santa Fe gave up its passenger service.

AMTRAK

By 1970, most of the railroads had given up passenger trains. The United States was faced with the possibility of almost no railroad passenger services.

The U.S. Government created a railroad passenger service called Amtrak. In 1971, Amtrak trains began to run.

Today, Amtrak passenger trains travel between many of the nation's largest cities. Amtrak trains travel over 24,500 miles (39,400 kilometers) of track. Amtrak has about 1,500 passenger cars and 350 **locomotives** (LO kuh MO tivz).

Amtrak's Empire Builder *races along near Glacier National Park, Montana. Amtrak trains have kept alive many of the famous names of old passenger trains.*

THE RISE AND FALL OF PASSENGER TRAINS

Before cars and airplanes, people in North America needed passenger trains for travel. Trains moved millions of passengers to and from towns large and small.

After World War II (1941-1945), people used their automobiles more and more. Beginning in the 1950s, airplanes also took many passengers away from American trains.

By 1958, most passenger railroads were losing money. The U.S. Government allowed these railroads to begin stopping their passenger service.

Streamlined steam engines were popular from the mid-1930s into the 1940s. Passenger trains in those days were still in demand.

FAMOUS PASSENGER TRAINS

All of America's intercity trains today are Amtrak trains. Before Amtrak, intercity trains were run by dozens of private railroads.

Some of those trains were fast and sleek. They offered great service and all the comforts of home. They were called streamliners. Among the most famous were Great Northern's *Empire Builder,* Santa Fe's *Chief,* and Pennsylvania's *Broadway Limited.*

New York Central ran the *Twentieth Century.* Northern Pacific had its *North Coast Limited.* Three streamliners written about in songs were Wabash's *Cannonball,* Seaboard's *Orange Blossom Special,* and Illinois Central's *City of New Orleans.*

14

The Burlington's stainless steel Nebraska Zephyr was one of the first diesel streamliners.

PASSENGER TRAINS TODAY

The great variety of passenger trains is gone. But Amtrak trains and Canada's VIA Rail carry more than 25,000,000 passengers each year. Commuter trains carry even more passengers than Amtrak. Many travelers depend on commuters for service from suburbs to such cities as Chicago and New York.

Commuter trains are cheap to ride and one commuter train can take the place of 1,000 automobiles. That helps save fuel and reduce air pollution.

Amtrak's intercity trains take passengers over old, scenic routes in new, lightweight cars. Here the Empire Builder *crosses the Flathead River in Western Montana.*

PASSENGER CARS

Most passenger cars are coaches. These cars have several rows of seats on one or two floors, but without tables, couches, or food service. Most commuter trains are made up of coach cars.

Some of the best intercity trains of the 1940s and 1950s included dining cars, sleeping cars, observation-lounge cars, and **dome** (DOM) cars, along with coaches.

A stainless steel observation car brings up the rear of CP Rail's Canadian in Ontario in 1970.

Dome cars were first used on trains in the 1940s. Dome cars have a second floor above the main level. Upstairs riders can view the passing countryside through huge glass windows.

Some of the finest passenger cars over the years were made by the Pullman Company of Chicago. A few old Pullmans are still used on special tour trains.

Today's Amtrak trains continue to carry a variety of passenger cars, including diners, sleepers, club, dome, and double-deck cars.

General Motors' famed E and F unit locomotives hauled passenger trains from 1939 into the 1990s.

PASSENGER LOCOMOTIVES

The first passenger train locomotives were steam powered. Steam locomotives remained popular in North America into the 1940s. By 1950, however, streamlined diesel-electric locomotives had replaced most North American steam power. Almost all trains today are pulled by diesel-electric locomotives.

The fastest of America's passenger trains, though, is the electric-powered Metroliner, between Washington, D.C., and New York.

The first true electric engines were built in the late 1800s.

GLOSSARY

commuter (kuh MEU ter) — passenger train that carries people between large cities and their suburbs

dome (DOM) — glass-covered area that is raised above the roofline of a railroad passenger car

intercity (IN ter SIT ee) — servicing or linking two or more cities

locomotive (LO kuh MO tiv) — power plant or engine on wheels used to push or pull railroad cars; a train engine

suburb (SUB erb) — small town or city that houses many people who work nearby in a big city

INDEX

FURTHER READING

Find out more about trains with these helpful books and information sites:
Riley, C.J. *The Encyclopedia of Trains and Locomotives.* Metro Books, 1995

Association of American Railroads online at www.aar.org
California State Railroad Museum online at www.csrmf.org
Union Pacific Railroad online at http://www.uprr.com